KING KONG JOKE BOOK

MOVIE STAR

JIM SIMON

Illustrations
Richard Dominguez

FutureRetro Entertainment
New York City

INTRODUCTION

By King Kong, "Super" Movie Star!

Hey, so how you doin'? Glad to meet you and all that jazz, and glad you're reading my book!

As you know, I am still the king of movies. My first starring-role movie, 1933's RKO *King Kong* left audiences screaming for more. Huge! I was just a young showbiz ape looking for a starring role, then suddenly I was a tremendous blockbuster — and so was the movie! Since then, the "Kong" — as I sometimes refer to myself — has gone super big-time Hollywood, starring in dozens of blockbuster movies worldwide. Today I am bigger and more popular than ever! And tomorrow, watch out!!

So my agent hired this nice author to write the Kong's very own unauthorized book. This book's *unauthorized* 'cause I refuse to pay the author. Hey, the Kong didn't hire the author to write this book, my agent did — so let my agent pay the guy, I say! You really have to watch yourself when dealing with these Hollywood types!!

I hope you enjoy my memoirs, which is what this

book is about. Some people who read it already kind of told me — in a quiet kind of way, as via a very, *very* long-distance phone call — this book is not really a memoir 'cause it's too funny, full of jokes! JOKES ABOUT ME! KING KONG! THE TOP SHOWBIZ BANANA!!

Listen, if you find this book is not really about my life in showbiz I'd truly appreciate you letting me know. Then I'll take this nice author up to the roof of the tallest skyscraper in New York City and throw him all the way to Skull Island!

Ok, ok, my agent is calling again. He says I gotta be on a plane for a movie shoot. Yeah, yeah, he says be on the plane 'cause there's no way I can fit inside the plane! My agent — he flies First Class, but me — I gotta cling to the outside of the plane for dear life or I'll fall like a cocoanut from a coconut tree and bang up my beautiful face! Like I said before: You really have to watch yourself when dealing with these Hollywood types!!!

P.S.: Hey, Tarz, grow some hair already!!

CONTENTS

KING "HOLLYWOOD" KONG

THE BEST AND THE WORST:
FUNNY STUFF JOKES

What did King Kong's girlfriend write on her Facebook page after spending the night with King Kong?

Dear Facebook friends: I have a problem…

***

What was King Kong doing on the Planet of the Apes?

Trying to figure out how to get out of there!

***

How can you keep King Kong's love?

By not returning it!

***

Why did King Kong climb to the top of the Empire State Building?

He had to catch a plane and couldn't get to the

airport on time!

***

How can you tell King Kong is in bed with you?

You can smell the bananas on his breath!

***

A man walking down a jungle path sees King Kong holding a Skull Crawler on an iron leash.

The man tops and says to Kong, "Does your Skull Crawler bite?"

Kong replies, "My Skull Crawler doesn't."

The man pats the Skull Crawler and has his hand bitten. "I thought you said your Skull Crawler doesn't bite," says the injured man."

"My Skull Crawler doesn't bite, says Kong.

"Look at my bloody arm!" the man yells.

"I don't know whose Skull Crawler *this one* belongs to," replies Kong, "but I *my* Skull Crawler doesn't bite!"

***

"HEY! NO TICKLIN' THE CAPTAIN UNDEROOS!"

How can you tell when King Kong is getting ready to charge?

When he takes out his credit card!

***

What do you call the stuff between King Kong's toes?

Slow people!

***

Why doesn't King Kong eat clowns?

Because they taste funny!

***

How did King Kong make the natives restless?

He put prune juice in their drinking water!

***

King Kong: "Hey, Godzilla, why are you wearing gym shorts?"

Godzilla: "It's my exercise day."

King Kong: "You're going to lift weights at the gym?"

Godzilla: "Don't be nuts! I'm going to knock down buildings in Tokyo!!"

***

Godzilla: "Hey, King Kong, why are you wearing gym sneakers?"

King Kong: "It's my exercise day."

Godzilla: "You're going to play basketball at the gym?"

King Kong: "Don't be nuts! I'm going to climb up tall buildings in New York City!!"

***

What kind of suit does King Kong wear?

A hirsute!

***

What did Godzilla have at the "All You Can Eat"

restaurant?

The waiters!

***

What was in King Kong's sandbox?

His pet camel!

***

Why did King Kong air-condition his hotel room?

Because he couldn't open the window!

***

King Kong walks into a store and asks the clerk, "Do you have any bananas?"

"No," the clerk says. This same thing happens the next day.

On the third day the clerk replies, "No, and if you come in asking for bananas again I will nail your hairy paws to the floor!"

On the next day King Kong walks in and asks,"

Got any nails?

"No," says the clerk.

"Got any bananas?" King Kong asks!

***

What could ruin King Kong's love-life?

The fear of height!

***

Why did King Kong want a girl with an hourglass figure?

Because he wanted a girl who could show him a good time!

***

What happens when King Kong sits in front of you at the movie theater?

You miss most of the movie!

***

If King Kong got married and had a baby boy, what would you call the baby?

Son of King Kong!

***

Why did King Kong call his friend Mighty Joe Young?

Because Joe Young never used deodorant!

***

What does King Kong hit when he goes to a bar?

He hits the bottle!

***

Where does King Kong go when he's sleepy?

He goes to bed!

***

If King Kong lived in glass house, what would he never open?

The curtains!

***

What is King Kong in New York City?

An urban guerilla!

***

A man walks into a bar with a T-Rex. "Give me a beer and give my friend a bucket of Fish 'n Chips," the man says.

The bartender serves the beer and gives the T-Rex a bucket of Fish 'n Chips. As the T-Rex devours the Fish 'n Chips, the bartender says, "Why is that T-Rex not as big as the T-Rex in the museum?"

The man says, "This T-Rex was created by scientists for the Jurassic Park movie and even though he's not the size of a real prehistoric T-Rex he is still big enough that he barely fits into the bar and he's meaner and tougher than any creature alive."

The man has a few drinks and asks the bartender if he wants to buy the T-Rex.

"What do I need a T-Rex for?"

"Watch this" the man says. "You see that loud-mouth bothering your customers at the end of the bar? T-Rex — Attack!"

The T-Rex goes over to the loud-mouth, smashes the daylights out of the guy and throws him out the door.

"Good T-Rex," the man says. "Now go sit down and eat your Fish 'n Chips." The T-Rex goes and sits in a corner.

The bartender asks "You mind if I give that a try?"

The man says, "No problem, go ahead."

The bartender sees a big tough drunk at the other end of the bar making trouble so he looks over and says, "T-Rex — Attack!"

T-Rex goes over and smashes the daylights out of the guy and throws him out the door."

Well the bartender buys the T-Rex and for months nobody makes the slightest bit of trouble. Then one day King Kong comes busting through the door making all kinds of noise and mayhem. The bartender yells, "T-Rex — Attack!"

T-Rex goes over and using its strong thighs,

powerful tail and its massive thick skull starts pounding on King Kong. King Kong is punching back and they're going at it blow by blow, wrecking the bar and each other. King Kong suddenly lands a tremendous series of punches knocking T-Rex's serrated teeth out of its mouth. They both go rolling out in the street. T-Rex claws and gorilla hair are getting torn off and dust is flying everywhere. The whole ground is shaking like an earthquake.

Finally King Kong comes strutting back into the bar, beating his fists against his chest, and says "Damn T-Rexes! Give 'em Fish 'n Chips and they think they're Godzilla!"

***

Why was King Kong so desperate to get off the Planet of the Apes?

He doesn't want to hang around with stinkin'apes!

***

How did the Grand Canyon form?

King Kong dropped his last dime!

***

Why did King Kong want to learn to write?

So he could send out lunch orders!

***

What did King Kong say when he saw a Picasso canvas?

"That looks like something a human would draw!"

***

How big is King Kong?

King Kong is so big that when he has a picture taken, the photographer charges him a group rate!

***

Did King Kong give his girlfriend a present?

No! He gave her a past!

***

"AS YOU CAN SEE, IN REAL LIFE I AM QUITE
SVELTE--IT'S THOSE MOVIE
CAMERAS THAT MAKE ME LOOK LIKE A
HUGE SCARY APE!!"

What happened when King Kong ate too much artificial sweetener?

He got an artificial toothache!

***

What happens when King Kong dances?

Earthquakes!

***

When did King Kong find himself in a soap opera?

When he was singing in the shower and shampoo got in his mouth!

***

What did the Martian say when he met King Kong?

"Don't take me to your barber!"

***

What song does King Kong sing when he gets drunk with his friends?

"The Gang's All Hair"!

***

Why did King Kong pick up the taxi-cab?

Because he's weird!

***

Why is King Kong's nightclub act dangerous?

Because he breaks up the audience!

***

How does King Kong know when it's going to rain?

He watches the TV weather report!

***

How does King Kong get lit up?

He sticks his finger into an electric socket!

***

What dance can King Kong do?

The stomp!

***

After ten days in town, what kind of party did everyone want to give King Kong?

A farewell party!

***

Why doesn't King Kong like to sleep on the Empire State Building's 13th floor?

Bad luck!

***

How do you hold King Kong?

At gunpoint!

***

What did actor Charlton Heston say when King Kong gave him a hug at the Hollywood Premier for the 1968 movie, The Planet of the Apes?

"Take your stinking paws off me you damn dirty ape!"

***

Why did King Kong get down on his knees?

He had to tie his tennis sneakers!

***

How does King Kong catch a Skull Crawler?

He digs a real deep hole in the ground then puts sugar all around the edge and when the Skull Crawler comes along and stops for eat the sugar, King Kong kicks it into the hole!

***

What is it when King Kong talks?

Monkey talk!

***

What's huge and hairy and climbs up buildings in a dress?

Queen Kong!

Why did King Kong jump into the Hudson River?

Because he wanted to visit New Jersey!

***

King Kong uses bed sheets for what?

Handkerchiefs!

***

When does King Kong know when he's been injured?

Just after he sees his lawyer!

***

What is King Kong afraid of turning into?

A big man in movies!

***

What does King Kong plan to do if his 350-horsepower car doesn't start?

Shoot it 350 times!

***

Tarzan's youngest daughter goes to her dad, who is working in the garden. She asks him, "Daddy, what is *sex*?"

Tarzan is surprised that she would ask such a question, but decides that if she is old enough to ask the question, then she is old enough to get an honest answer — the same way Jane explained it to him years ago.

So he starts to tell his daughter all about the "birds and the bees". When he finishes explaining, the little girl is looking at him with her mouth hanging open. Tarzan askes her, "Why did you ask this question?"

His young daughter says, "Mom told me to tell you that dinner would be ready in just a couple of *secs*."

***

If you stood beside King Kong in an air-conditioned room, what would you get?

A cold shoulder!

***

Who put holes in King Kong's favorite shirt?

Mothra!

***

Who does King Kong visit twice a year since he started brushing with an electric toothbrush?

His electrician!

***

How does King Kong get high?

He climbs the Empire State Building!

***

Where does King Kong go?

Anywhere he wants!

***

What does King Kong do with the hole in a bagel?

He puts a banana through it!

***

Why does King Kong go to the bank?

He's got some interest there!

***

Why did King Kong take a cold tablet?

He wanted to cool off!

***

Why did King Kong climb the Empire State Building?

He wanted to use the front door, but they wouldn't let him in without a tie and jacket!

***

Why did King Kong have a glass mattress?

So he could make sure no one scary was hiding under his bed!

***

If you hid King Kong in a bell what would you have?

A ding-dong King Kong!

***

Tarzan: "Kong, get a haircut!"

Kong: "Tarzan, grown some hair!"

***

What are King Kong's three biggest fears?

- Public speaking to a crowd in New York City!

- Dancing with Tarzan!

- Godzilla showing up at King Kong's wedding!

***

Q: WHAT DID *KING KONG* GIVE THE PSYCHIATRIST?

A: "SHOCK TREATMENT!!"

How do you make King Kong laugh?

Tell him a Tarzan joke!

***

Why did King Kong dip pickles in yellow paint?

Because he wanted sour bananas!

***

How do you make King Kong cry?

Give him a mirror!

***

King Kong needed to go on a diet so he called a company and ordered their 5-day, 20 pound weight loss program.

The next day, there's a knock on the door and there stands before him a voluptuous, athletic, young woman dressed in nothing but a pair of running shoes and a sign around her neck.

She introduces herself as a representative of the

diet company. The sign reads, "If you catch me, you can have me."

Without a thought, Kong takes off after her. A mile later exhausted, he finally gives up. The same girl shows up for the next four days and the same thing happens. On the fifth day, he weighs himself and is delighted to find he has lost 20 pounds as promised.

He calls the company and again orders their 5-day/20 pound weight loss program. The next day there's a knock at the door and there stands the most beautiful young woman he has ever seen in his life. She is wearing nothing but running shoes and a sign around her neck that reads, "If you catch me you can have me forever".

Suddenly, he's out the door chasing after her. This young woman is in great shape and Kong does his best, but fails to catch her. So for the next 5 days, the same routine happens — with him gradually getting in better and better shape as a result.

Much to his delight on the seventh day when he weighs himself, he discovers that he has lost another 20 pounds. He calls the diet company yet again and orders the 10-day/40 pound weight loss program.

The diet company representative warns Kong on the phone. "This is our most difficult weight loss program. Are you really sure you can handle it?" Kong replies, "I haven't felt this amazing in years. Send it over here quick!"

A few days later there's a knock at the door. Full of excitement, Kong opens the door but instead of another beautiful athletic young woman, Kong finds Godzilla standing there wearing nothing but pink running shoes and a sign around his neck that reads, "If I catch you, you are mine."

That week, Kong lost 40 pounds and a couple of teeth but at least the engagement ring on his hairy finger looked nice!

***

Why did King Kong stuff his mattress with toasters?

So he could pop out of bed in the morning!

***

Why does King Kong get seven years bad luck

whenever he looks in the mirror?

Because whenever he looks in the mirror, the mirror-glass cracks!

***

How do you stop King Kong from snoring?

Stick ear plugs-in *your* ears!

***

What was King Kong when he was born?

A chimp off the old block!

***

What did King Kong give the psychiatrist?

Shock treatment!

***

It's so hot in the jungle, what does King Kong read to cool off?

Fan mail!

***

Where would you never think of finding King Kong if he had to hide?

In a barber shop!

***

What's sufficient ground for divorce from King Kong?

Marriage!

***

Why did King Kong join the Army?

To teach gorilla warfare!

***

What is King Kong's favorite form of government?

A banana republic!

***

Why did King Kong buy a 10-foot steel cable?

He needed a leash to walk his pet Skull Crawler!

***

Why did Tarzan find bowling balls in the top of the banana-tree?

King Kong always hides his bowling balls with his bananas!

***

When a King Kong develops chronic diarrhea, what do the natives do?

Run!

***

What goes Bam Bam Bam every Easter Day?

King Kong in his Easter bunny suit hopping across the lawn!

***

What is the reason King Kong uses a hammer?

For breaking pimples!

***

How did King Kong's son know King Kong used his comb?

He didn't—King Kong combs his hair with a tree branch!

***

What's faster than a speeding bullet, more powerful than a rushing locomotive, and able to leap tall buildings with a single bound?

King Kong Kangaroo!

***

Why did King Kong paint the bottoms of his feet brown when he saw Tarzan coming?

So that he could hide upside down in a jar of peanut butter!

***

Then there was the scientist who taught King Kong to play basketball...

Only problem was finding big enough basketball

sneakers!

***

What's the fastest thing in a wheelchair?

King Kong's grandmother with a nurse chasing her!

***

Why does King Kong get heartburn after every meal?

He has to digest the spears and shields of the natives that he eats!

***

How do you stop King Kong from overcharging?

Take away his credit cards!

***

What do you call King Kong's family shield mounted on the wall of his house?

His hairy coat of arms!

***

What goes "CHOMP CHOMP CHOMP, TIMBER!"

King Kong Termite!

***

Why did King Kong's girlfriend slap King Kong on the first date?

He was double clutching!

***

Describe the chief of the natives on King Kong's island.

Scared!

***

What eats a hundred bananas in 10 minutes?

Teenage King Kong!

***

How does King Kong get in shape?

He does ballet dancing!

***

Who made a monkey out of Tarzan?

King Kong when he played with Tarzan!

***

What does King Kong fear most?

Hair loss!

***

What knocks down little old ladies and steals their bread?

King Kong Pigeon!

***

King Kong: "Doc, each time I raise my arm it hurts!"

Doctor: "Well, don't raise your arm!"

***

What's the best way to wreck a house?

Rent it to King Kong's family!

***

How does King Kong get high?

He stands up straight!

***

How do you bug King Kong?

Hide a transmitter in his ear!

***

When King Kong can't make up his mind, what is he?

Kong-**fused**!

***

Kong: "Tarzan, why do you wear that loincloth?"

Tarzan: "For protection from far-sighted banana pickers who lost their eyeglasses!"

***

Professor: I read recently that over 865,000 people died last year from malnutrition--and King Kong gained weight!

Student: But does King Kong count?

Professor: If he's smart, he does!

***

What eats three porterhouse steaks, six pounds of vegetables, twelve gallons of milk for supper, and wakes everyone in the middle of the night?

King Kong's baby!

***

What sounds like an erupting volcano?

King Kong burping!

***

Why doesn't King Kong swim every day?

It takes a week for his hair to dry!

***

Reporter: "Are you satisfied with your role as one of the world's top action heroes?"

King Kong: "Sure…but I need a vacation…"

Reporter: "How about a two-week cruise to Barbados?"

King Kong: "How about a weekend in New York City…!"

***

What's louder than a fire siren, early in the morning?

King Kong Rooster!

***

Why did King Kong's girlfriend break up with him?

She felt he was always looking down on her!

***

Why did King Kong wear hiking boots to the basketball game?

He couldn't find his sneakers!

***

Why does King Kong pick up elephants?

Because he's *really* weird!

***

When King Kong's parrot says, "Polly wants a cracker!" what do you do?

YOU GIVE THE PARROT A CRACKER!

***

Did the King Kong have a brother?

No, but he had a lot of monkey uncles!

***

When did the police know the bank robber was King Kong?

When they found him holding up the bank.

***

How do you shake hands with King Kong?

Very carefully!

***

Why does King Kong go to a psychiatrist?

To talk to someone!

***

What keeps King Kong running?

Too much fiber!

***

Why was King Kong's girlfriend so upset when he came into her bedroom?

Because he forgot to open the door before he came into her room!

***

When does King Kong run in slow motion?

When his sneakers are too small!

***

Why did King Kong swim across the Atlantic Ocean to Brazil?

Because Brazil has really good bananas!

***

What does King Kong do when he can't sleep on an empty stomach?

He sleeps on his back!

***

When happened when King Kong joined the army?

He knocked himself unconscious every time he saluted the sergeant!

***

What does King Kong have in his bathroom?

The super bowl!

***

Why did the doctor move King Kong's nose to the middle of his face?

Because that's Kong's scenter!

***

What doe King Kong call a tough but beautiful French woman?

Piece de resistance!

***

What time is it when King Kong drives through your garage?

Time to get a new garage!

"WHAT DO YOU MEAN--I HAVE A FACE
ONLY A *MOTHRA* COULD LOVE?!!"

***

What should you get when you're run over by King Kong?

His license plate!

If you put several of King Kong's ducks in a box, what do you have?

A box of King Kong's quackers!

***

What should King Kong's plumber be?

Toilet trained!

***

What lies on the bottom of the ocean and shakes?

A nervous Godzilla!

***

Why can King Kong see so well in the dark?

Because he eats lots of carrots with his bananas!

***

How does King Kong tell your fortune?

By reading banana leaves!

***

Why was King Kong ticketed for driving on the interstate highway?

Because he was driving an elephant!

***

Godzilla speaking to King Kong: "Who died and made you king?!"

***

King Kong speaking to Godzilla: "Stop eating so much Fish 'n Ships!"

***

How long did King Kong have bad eye -sight?

Until he got a haircut!

***

Is it unhealthy to kiss King Kong's girlfriend?

It is if King Kong is around!

***

How small is King Kong's hometown?

It's so small that when King Kong comes to visit there's no room for anyone else!

***

Will King Kong attack you if you carry a newspaper?

It depends on how fast you carry the newspaper!

***

What is King Kong doing when he walks around the block?

Monkeying around!

***

How should you dress when meeting King Kong?

We don't know-but don't wear a yellow suit!

***

What caused 50 cars to slide into each other on the interstate highway?

King Kong dropped a banana peel at the toll booth!

***

Why did King Kong climb to the top of the Empire State Building?

He wanted a room with a view!

***

Why did King Kong build a pent house on the top of the Empire State Building?

He wanted a *bigger* room with a better view!

***

How small was King Kong's hotel room in

Hollywood?

King Kong's hotel room was so small that when he dropped his handkerchief, he had wall-to-wall carpeting!

***

When King Kong doesn't get his way, what does he get?

Bananas!

***

If King Kong won the lottery what would he have?

Monkey money!

***

What cruel joke did King Kong play on Tarzan?

He greased the vine!

***

Who is the biggest stripper in New York City?

King Kong peeling a banana on 42nd street!

***

Why did King Kong wear running shoes to the dance?

Because he couldn't find his tap shoes!

***

Why did King Kong knock down a building when he met Godzilla?

Monkey see, monkey do!

***

How do you stop King Kong from burping?

Hold him over your shoulder!

***

Who is the world's most feared coward?

King Kong, the hairy chicken!

***

What does King Kong's tailor make?

Monkey suits!

***

How do you make King Kong fast?

Don't feed him!

***

What does King Kong do when he gets fleas?

Scratches!

***

Why doesn't King Kong shave?

Because he doesn't know where to begin!

***

If King Kong put a banana peel under Sigmund Freud, what would you call it?

A Freudian slip!

***

What did King Kong do when he saw His girlfriend?

He went ape!

***

What boat did King Kong cross the ocean on?

A banana boat!

***

What do you call the woman who marries King Kong?

Mrs. King Kong when you first meet her, and later you call her Queen Kong!

***

THE INNER MIND OF *KING KONG*

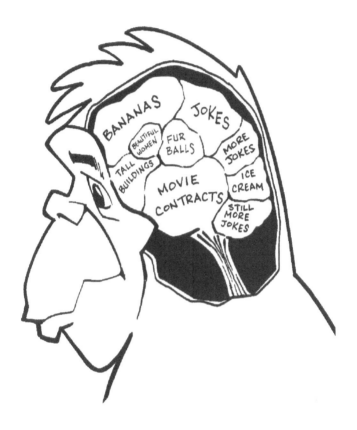

What's funnier than King Kong in a bathing suit?

King Kong in a bikini!

***

What do King Kong's teammates get when he hogs the ball?

Snorting mad!

***

Why did King Kong go to the dry cleaner?

Because he didn't want to get wet!

***

What does King Kong do when he goes to a party?

He crashes it!

***

How do you get King Kong to kiss you?

First you rub your body with bananas . . .

***

What did Tarzan say when he saw a herd of elephants with King Kong?

"Look! A herd of elephants!"

What did Tarzan say when he saw a herd of elephants with sunglasses?

Nothing — He didn't recognize them!

***

Tarzan and King Kong were relaxing in Tarzan's jungle bar when King Kong asked Tarzan if he wanted to play a round of pokers. "No way," said Tarzan. "Too many cheetahs here!"

***

Why didn't King Kong's girlfriend keep a picture of King Kong in her wallet?

Her wallet wasn't big enough for King Kong's picture!

***

Does King Kong play a fair game of ping pong?

Only if you watch him!

***

Why doesn't King Kong go to the park?

He's afraid of pigeons!

***

What kind of management did Godzilla's agent demand Godzilla get?

Anger management!

***

What do you call King Kong after he puts his arm in Godzilla's mouth!

Lefty!

***

How does King Kong pick his friends?

To pieces!

***

When does King Kong get down on his knees?

When he shoots marbles!

***

How do you fire King Kong?

You don't! You just keep giving him raises until he has enough money to start his own business!

***

Why do girls fall at King Kong's feet?

One look at him and they pass out with fear!

***

If King Kong makes a fortune in movie, what should you give him?

An accountant!

***

King Kong walks into Tarzan's restaurant, orders three super-sized hamburgers with extra-big fries and milkshakes and starts eating them as fast as he can.

Tarzan asks, "Hey, why are you eating so fast?"

King Kong says, "You would be eating fast, too, if you had what I had."

Tarzan asks, "What do you have?"

King Kong says, "Not enough money to pay."

***

Why did King Kong fall in love with his girlfriend?

They first time he saw her, she was wearing a fur coat and he thought she was a sexy, girl gorilla!

***

What's a hairy tent?

King Kong's fur coat!

***

What is King Kong's favorite week?

Be Kind to Animals Week!

***

When do you give King Kong a going-away present?

When you want him to go away!

***

What did King Kong say when he pulled open Godzilla's jaws?

Don't worry, I'm also a dentist!

***

When did King Kong see the handwriting on the wall?

When he went to the restroom!

***

Why couldn't King Kong add 7+5?

Because his pocket calculator broke!

***

How long did it take King Kong to cross the ocean?

About as long as it took him to drive cross-town in New York City!

***

When King Kong goes to the barber, does he always get a haircut?

No! He gets *all* of them cut!

***

What was King Kong's biggest trouble in New York City?

Finding a place to park his elephant!

***

When not working, King Kong gives his agent 10% of his unemployment check!

***

What did King Kong get for father's day?

A father!

***

What does King Kong put on for Halloween?

A human suit!

***

How do you shake hands with King Kong?

Very carefully!

***

What does King Kong use a belt for?

His wristwatch!

***

Q: WHAT DOES *KING KONG* SING WHEN HE GETS TOGETHER WITH FRIENDS?
A: "THE GANG'S ALL HAIR . . !"

Why should you never hit King Kong when he's down?

Because he might get up!

**

Why won't King Kong send air-mail letters?

Because every time he licks the stamp, he gets air-sick!

**

What was King Kong's job when he worked at the car wash?

Lifeguard!

**

Why does King Kong talk with his hands?

Because he's got bad breath!

**

How can you tell King Kong from his sister?

King Kong is the one *without* the mustache!

***

What happened when the waiter dropped the drinks on King Kong?

It was the first time the drinks were on a gorilla!

***

What does King Kong do with crumbs at his table?

He lets them stay there!

***

Why does King Kong want to get rid of red china?

Because it clashes with his purple tablecloth!

***

How did King Kong bite himself on his behind?

He sat on his false teeth!

***

Why did King Kong have so many cavities?

The coconuts he ate put holes in his teeth!

***

Why didn't King Kong's seven-day diet work?

Because he ate it all in one meal!

***

What is the floor show at King Kong's hotel?

Mice!

***

What would you get if you crossed King Kong with a roach?

We don't know — but you'd better not step on it!

***

Why does King Kong believe carrots are good for his eyes/

Because he's never seen a rabbit with glasses!

***

When does King Kong's girlfriend try to break down his door?

When he locks her in his bedroom!

***

When should you never slap King Kong in the face?

When he's chewing tobacco!

***

What happened when King Kong took a midnight stroll in New York City?

He got mugged!

***

What does King Kong order for Godzilla when they go to their favorite restaurant in London?

Fish 'n Ships!

***

Where does Tarzan wash his loincloth?

Usually in the back and front!

***

What did they make King Kong do when he drew a line three blocks long at his movie?

They made him erase it!

***

What does King Kong do when he has indigestion?

He belches!

***

What does King Kong use to put up a good front?

A bra!

***

What did King Kong say after he ate the drunken French explorer?

"That was the best French food I ever tasted!"

***

Why didn't King Kong speak to his girlfriend while they were watching the movie?

He didn't want to interrupt her!

***

What do you have when you give King Kong a piggy back ride?

A monkey on your back!

***

If you were King Kong's brother and he had a baby boy, what would that make you?

A monkey's uncle!

***

Can King Kong have a kid?

No — Goats have kids!

***

If King Kong went to medical school, what would he study?

Nothing — They'd study him!

***

When King Kong goes drinking with his friends, why do they make him drive home?

Because he's too drunk to sing!

***

If King Kong's new movie is a hit, what would you call him?

A top banana (eater)!

***

What goes best with a yellow polka dot tie on King

Kong?

Sunglasses!

***

Why did King Kong buy a suit?

Because he wanted to be a lawyer!

***

Why doesn't King Kong wear stockings?

Because they wrinkle around his knees!

***

Why did King Kong buy an amplifier for his wristwatch?

Because he wanted to be sure it could tell time!

***

Why does King Kong go to sleep at night?

So he can wake up in the morning!

***

Why doesn't King Kong learn to talk?

Because he gets everything he wants just by growling!

***

Why won't King Kong eat peanuts?

Because he's never seen a skinny elephant!

***

When King Kong was asked to write his autobiography, what did he title it?

KING KONG'S AUTOBIOGRAPHY!

***

What hand does King Kong use to stir his coffee?

Neither — He uses a spoon!

***

What happened when King Kong ran away with the circus?

The police made him bring it back!

***

Why was King Kong overjoyed when the landlord said he would raise the rent?

Because King Kong was having a hard time raising the rent himself!

***

If King Kong had one wish, what would it be?

To yell back at Tarzan!

***

Why did the barber drop a hot towel on King Kong's face?

Because he didn't want to burn his fingers!

Q: WHY DID *KING KONG* GO ON A DIET?
A: SO HE COULD FIT IN HIS NEW CAR!!

***

Before walking into an occupied bedroom, what does King Kong do?

He peeks through the keyhole!

**

What did King Kong look like in Alaska?

A blue gorilla!

***

There's so much pollution in New York City, King Kong doesn't water his banana trees…

He dusts them!

***

Why did New York City take away King Kong's breath?

Because the air pollution was so bad, he couldn't breathe!

***

Why does King Kong feel at home in front of New York City audiences?

Coming from the jungle, he's used to savages!

***

What does King Kong wear in a nudist camp?

Nothing — he just shaves closely!

***

How did King Kong make it to the top in Hollywood?

He climbed the tallest building in Hollywood!

***

Why would King Kong rather be poor than rich?

Because being poor is cheaper!

***

What does King Kong get when he breaks out in his new movie?

A rash!

***

When did King Kong fall for His girlfriend?

When he slipped off the Empire State Building!

***

Why did King Kong take a sleeping pill with a reducing pill?

Because he wanted to take a light nap!

***

Why does King Kong have trouble telephoning China?

He keeps getting Wong numbers!

***

Why did King Kong tell his girlfriend to put on

lipstick?

Because she was so small — he needed a target!

***

When was King Kong like a wolf?

When King Kong's girlfriend was wearing a sweater and he tried to pull the wool over her eyes!

***

Why did King Kong wear dark glasses?

So no one would recognize him!

***

How did King Kong save $20,000?

His girlfriend didn't show up for their wedding!

***

What passes out with New Year's Eve?

King Kong, after drinking one too many!

***

What does King Kong do about cracks in subways?

He refuses to laugh!

***

At what kind of work does King Kong do a bang-up job?

Parking cars!

***

How cheap was King Kong's hotel?

The hotel was so cheap — the bellboy stole towels *from* King Kong!

***

When does it snow in summer?

When King Kong gets dandruff in July!

***

What would you get if you crossed King Kong with a kangaroo?

King Kong with pockets!

***

What does King Kong do with trees?

He puts the trees in his tennis sneakers to stretch his sneakers!

***

Why did King Kong get all choked up?

Because someone starched his underwear!

***

Why doesn't a monkey argue with King Kong?

Because the monkey is afraid Kong will make a man out of him!

***

Why did King Kong give up dancing?

It got too expensive to keep repairing the floor!

***

What was King Kong's slogan when he worked as a cook?

All Food Is Untouched By Human Hands!

***

What did King Kong's girlfriend tell everyone after their first date?

"My boyfriend is an animal!"

***

Why is it a lucky thing King Kong is not a lion?

Ask the lion!

***

When King Kong came to New York City, why did he feel at home?

Because he went from a jungle to a jungle!

***

What did King Kong say to the bouncer when he walked into the bar?

"Don't worry — I'm over 21!"

***

If you crossed King Kong with an elephant, what would you get?

Something hairy that never forgets!

***

Why did the movie producer give King Kong's girlfriend a 12-foot pole?

Because she said she wouldn't touch King Kong with a ten-foot pole!

***

Why did the movie producer plant a banana tree in King Kong's living room?

To keep King Kong off the streets at night!

***

Can you hear King Kong playing the piano?

Not if the piano is broken!

***

Was King Kong raised by the book?

Yes! The Bronx Zoo Book!

***

At King Kong's movie, what was the door prize?

The door!

***

When do you know King Kong has a big mouth?

When he eats a human sideways!

***

Is King Kong's girlfriend a music lover?

No! She's an animal lover!

***

Can King Kong play piano by ear?

He can if he gets a haircut!

***

What did King Kong do with Beethoven's Fifth?

He drank it!

***

Why does playing the accordion make King Kong cry like a baby?

Because it keeps pinching his belly!

***

How slow was business at King Kong's nightclub?

Business was so slow — the bouncer was arrested for loitering!

Q: WHY DOES *KING KONG* PICK UP TAXIS?
A: BECAUSE HE'S WEIRD!!

Why does King Kong's wife wear pink suspenders?

To hold up her purple girdle!

***

Why did King Kong take the tailor to the top of the Empire State Building?

He wanted to see if the tailor measured up!

***

What's the worst thing about climbing up the Empire State Building?

Climbing back down!

***

How tough is King Kong?

King Kong is so tough…he eats tuna fish without removing the can!

***

What steps would you take if King Kong cornered you in a dark alley?

Long and fast ones!

***

What does the sign say in King Kong's favorite bar?

Nothing — Signs can't speak!

***

What's King Kong with cotton is his mouth?

A big mumbling ape!

***

How did King Kong make a killing in the market?

He accidentally stepped on his stockbroker!

***

What kind of pig did King Kong ignore at his birthday party?

A wild bore!

***

Why did King Kong want to attend school in Hollywood?

Because he wanted to study the stars!

***

Why did King Kong bring a six pack of bananas to the Supreme Court?

He wanted to make a federal case out of it!

***

Why did King Kong take his girlfriend to the top of the Empire State Building?

She had already been to the top of the Statue of Liberty!

***

Why did King Kong's girlfriend kiss him on the lips?

Someone put her up to it!

***

When did King Kong know he was getting closer to the heart of New York City?

When he realized he was stepping on more and more people!

***

Why did King Kong keep falling out of the tree?

Because he built his treehouse upside down!

***

Where does King Kong take out his dinner?

To the garbage!

***

Why did King Kong order prescription windows?

So he could have a clearer view!

***

Why is King Kong a great actor?

Because whenever he enters a nightclub, he brings down the house!

***

What does King Kong get when he strains his back?

A monkey wrench!

***

What is it called when King Kong gets the flu?

The King Kong Flu!

***

Why did King Kong drive his new car off the cliff?

He wanted to test the air brakes!

***

Why doesn't King Kong ride the subways?

He can't fit through the turnstiles!

***

What did King Kong's agent say when the ape fell off the Empire State Building?

"Another smash hit!"

***

Why did King Kong walk around in circles?

Because he nailed one of his feet to the floor!

***

What did the stream say when King Kong sat in it?

"I'll be damned!"

***

What did King Kong say when his ship hit an iceberg?

"Who ordered ice?"

***

What is bigger than King Kong and is weightless?

King Kong's shadow!

***

Two Skull Island cannibals are sitting around eating a clown. One cannibal says to the other, "Does this taste funny to you?"

***

What never asks King Kong a question yet must be answered?

King Kong's phone!

***

How did King Kong make sure there were no chicks in his eggs?

He bought duck eggs!

***

Why did King Kong buy a dog to go to California?

He saw a sign that said "Go Greyhound!"

***

Why is King Kong a square?

He goes to hotels—and sleeps in them!

***

How late does King Kong like to stay out in Paris?

Until the very oui hours of morning!

***

Tarzan: "King Kong is so rich from his movies that he rides his own motorcycle!"

Godzilla: "Big deal! A lot of people ride their own motorcycle."

Tarzan: "In their living room?!"

***

When did King Kong throw away his hearing aid?

After he got a haircut!

***

When did King Kong finally break out?

When he ate a case of strawberries!

***

Why did King Kong wear a pink sweater?

Because his blue sweater was in the wash!

***

Why did King Kong go to Miami?

To get a suntan!

***

What did King Kong do when forgot to wear his eyeglasses at the opening night of his new movie?

He mistook a Yellow Cab for a banana, picked it up, peeled it and ate the WHOLE thing…!

***

KING KONG INTERVIEW

Hello. My name's King Kong …

Actually, I'm not the original King Kong. There were two or three Kongs before me…but who's counting…?

You think it's easy being the second or third King Kong? I work hard. I'm not just monkeying around…

I got into show biz by doing impressions…but only the big acts…

I used to lead safaris into deepest Africa…That wasn't easy, working out of Hoboken, New Jersey….

People wonder why I climbed the George Washington Bridge…I simply got tired of climbing the Empire State Building…

***

The movie studio wanted to dig up my original girlfriend for a new King Kong movie...I told my agent, "NO WRAY!"

***

KING KONG AT SARDI'S

Since the 1920s, Sardi's in NYC's Theater District has been a legendary "star-gazing" restaurant and bar. Famous for its caricatures of showbiz celebrities lining the walls, Sardi's is one of Kong's favorite places.

Kong: Bartender! Another drink!

Bartender: No more for you Kong — Go Home and sleep it off...

Kong: Says who!

Bartender: Says my bouncer — the guy's an ape!

Kong: Another ape? I'll buy him a drink!!!

Bartender: Listen, whaddaya wanna drink so much for?

Kong: I'm homesick…couple more drinks and I'll start seeing elephants again!

Bartender: Well…I guess a few more drinks can't hurt…

Kong: My Daddy used to say drinking would put hair on my chest…He never lied….

Bartender: Aw…here's your drink, Kong — It will make a man outta you!

Kong: And ruin my act…? I'm going home….!!!

***

BANANAS, KONG!!!

"Mother, can I play the piano?"

"Bananas, Kong! Your claws will scratch the ivories!!!

***

"But dad, I don't need a haircut!"

"Bananas, Kong! Comb your face!!!"

***

"Gosh, this is a lovely dress!"

"Bananas, Kong! Give it back to my girlfriend before she catches cold!!!"

***

"Hey, sweetheart, you want to see the town tonight?"

"Bananas, Kong! If you climb up that sky-scraper again, I'll scream!!!"

***

"Kong, quit pulling that girl's arm!"

"Kong, quit pulling that girl's arm!"

"Bananas, Kong! Give that girl back her arm!!!"

***

"Mom, can I go with you to the supermarket?"

"Bananas, Kong! You know you can't fit in the Volkswagen!!!"

***

"Sir, I just pulled your daughter out of the pond and resuscitated her!"

"Bananas, Kong! Now, quick, get her some mouthwash!!!"

***

"Mom...gurgle, gurgle, gurgle, gurgle, gurgle..."

"Bananas, Kong! How many times have I told you not to speak with someone in your mouth!?!"

***

"Ma'am, I just stepped on your husband!"

"Bananas, King! Slip him under the door!!!"

***

LOVE LETTERS FROM CAMP

Dear Mumsy and Popsy:

Just a note to let you know that I've finally met Mr. Right! It happened several days ago at that marvelous summer camp you sent me to! His name is Kong, but his friends call him King! And rightly so, since he's tall, dark and hairy!!!

Kong is a musician, but works here as a counselor to earn extra money. He's a nature specialist. You know — chest pounding, tree climbing, all that sort of stuff! Well, mumsy and popsy, it was faint-hearted love at first sight. First sight of Kong, I fainted!!! I knew he loved me, but he was so shy: A couple of grunts, bananas sent to my bunkhouse… Oh, how romantic!

We plan to visit soon. I hope the guest room is painted. (Yellow is Kong's favorite color!) We'll probably live at home until a job opens up. Kong, of course, is a little worried about the employment situation back in the States. I told him the streets of America are paved with gold. "Yes," he said, "but are there bananas?" Oh, what a wonderful sense of humor! And tell junior, Kong builds the most adorable treehouses!

So, mumsy and popsy, I hope to see you all very soon. I have to go now: Kong is working on our music act and I have to lift the piano while he plays!!!

Love and Kisses,
King Kong's Girlfriend

**

Dear Maw and Paw:

WOW! I just met this really amazing mate in summer camp! I call her Sweetheart, but because she's from a very wealthy family she uses the alias "Wealthy Sweetheart."

Anyway, it looks now like we'll be swinging together! She wants me to meet her parents. I don't know... I think that instead of getting serious, I'd rather monkey around with her!!! What should I do? The girl's driving me bananas!

Well, maw and paw, tell Cheetah and Tarzan goodbye for me. Please break the news gently to Tarzan, as you know how these things drive him up a tree! And please don't forget to change the peanut oil in my elephant!

> Love and bananas,
> King Kong

***

GORILLA GOSSIP

King Kong might be a big ape, but he's one gorilla who knows how to pick up women...says a great place to pick up blondes is at the Empire State Building, top floor....

***

Talking about his former girlfriend, Kong reported "she was a great kid who might have screamed if I didn't bring home the bananas, but I had her just where I wanted her — in the palm of my paw!"....

***

Kong's nightclub act said to be going full guns...plays hit song "BEAUTIFUL DREAMER" forwards and backwards... When asked how he learned to play "Beautiful Dreamer" backwards, Kong replied "It's easy....first you turn around the piano stool...."

***

OVERHEARD AT THE EMPIRE STATE BUILDING

Reporter: "Mr. Kong, what's your impression of the Big Apple now that you're here for a second visit?"

Kong: "It's a great place to visit if you don't want to live…."

***

A BIG APE, A REALLY BIG APE

See, there's this guy named Carl Denham. And this Carl character is in the movie business. Well, one day some drunken sailor tells him about an exotic island filled with monsters and prehistoric creatures. Sounds like a possible quickie but goodie budget film location, thinks Carl. And so he gets the cameras rolling. And has all these great ideas for a terrific plot. And orders champagne. And rants raving mad down Broadway in only his jockey shorts. And…Well, let's let Carl tell it in his own words….

"I'll tell you what I wanted to do...I wanted to make a movie about an ape that falls in love with a girl...Or a girl who falls in love with an ape...Does it really matter?!?....

Anyway, I got a great idea–Africa! It wasn't so easy after that...Well, as it turned out, I hired a crew and ship...The ship was docked in New York City's harbor...But I couldn't sail until morning...at high sewage....

All night I paced the streets of Gotham...I needed a girl...I had this great idea for a movie and no girl...I racked my brains for a lead, bemoaning my fate...This city is filled with big apes — a dime a dozen — but pretty girls???

Then suddenly, I chanced upon a shop owner accusing a girl of stealing an apple...The guy looked just like New York City's Mayor...He was yelling, "That girl! That girl, she's taking too big a-bit outta the Big Apple...!

Of course I came to the girl's aid...She nearly fainted in my brutish, hairy arms.

"I love hairy arms," she sighed.

"If you love hairy arms, have I got a gorilla for you!!!" I told her.

She was half starved and very beautiful...I sneaked her into my cabin, whispering into her ear, "I've got a job for you — money, adventure and fame, the thrill of a lifetime...and a long, long voyage...."

The ship journeyed for a very long time...My girlfriend asked, nibbling at my ear, "What ocean is this, darling?"

"A very large and deep ocean," I replied.

"It must be a specific ocean," she cooed, dabbing a cotton swab on the bloody pulp which was once my ear.

"All right, it's the Specific Ocean...."

Later, on deck, I confided in my first mate, Driscoll, about the girl.

"Does this mean it's over for us?" Driscoll wanted

to know….

"Did you ever hear of Kong?" I asked the crew.

"No," some rummy said, "but if you hum a few bars, we can try to sing it…"

Captain Englehorn had heard the word, though…He stepped forward…fell off the ship….

"Denham!" he called to me. "The word refers to some spirit or creature, neither man nor beast! Something all-powerful, still living…holding Skull Island in a grip of fear!!!"

As I watched Captain Englehorn drift away to the horizon, I thought how lucky it was that I had brought along an extra supply of underarm deodorant….

The following morning, the fog lifted…The ship approached Skull Island…I organized a landing party…"Last one on shore's a monkey's uncle!" I shouted, diving head-first into the shallow water….

On the island, we were greeted by a strange, awesome sight…A band of natives were pounding beer bottles on tables, calling "Kong!...Kong!..."

I decided right then and there to bring Kong back to America! If he could do this to the natives, imagine how he'd bring down the house with the out-of-towners! Never had I seen an ape get such an encore...Already, visions of a 25-per-cent agent's fee were dancing in my head — But at that very moment, a group of natives were kidnapping a beautiful young woman from the ship...!!

The natives dragged her to the Great Wall...The whole thing was a real drag...She was tied to a stone column...The natives retreated beyond the locked gates! Then, as she struggled to get free, a thundering, crashing noise erupted from the jungle....

"Who's that!" the young woman wondered...Hugh Hefner in a monkey suit? She hoped this didn't mean another centerfold — those staples just took too much out of her!!!

And that's when Kong exposed himself! She screamed that he'd better zip up his pants fast — before the movie gets an R rating!!!

"Oh boy," Kong blubbered, "a new Barbie Doll…!" The last one the natives gave him was a dud — it was a Ken Doll!

It was at the same moment that the movie crew and I broke through the gates.

"Smile," I shouted, popping a flash, "you're on America's Funniest Home Videos TV Show!"

I demanded to know what that big gorilla wanted with the girl. Kong answered that he had a thing for blondes.

"Well you'd better keep it to yourself," I shouted back, snapping an 8x10 glossy….

"Blondes," I laughed. "What makes you think she's not a brunette or redhead…!

"Only her hairdresser knows for sure!" replied Kong, taking the woman in his hand…er…paw.

"Get your hairy paw off that lady, you male chauvinist ape!" I shouted.

But Kong paid no mind to us as he carried off the

world's most beautiful young woman into the darkness of deepest Africa…Which all goes to prove: blondes really do have more fun…!!!"

***

WHY I NEVER MARRIED MY SWEETHEART

by

King Kong, World's Biggest Author

1: I never married my sweetheart because she demanded custody of the bananas!

***

2: I never married my sweetheart because we could never slip into motels without being noticed!

***

3: I never married my sweetheart because she insisted I shave me legs!

***

4: I never married my sweetheart because I insisted she shave her legs!

***

5: I never married my sweetheart because how would I explain it to Tarzan?!!!

***

6: I never married my sweetheart because she was an atheist and didn't believe in Godzilla!

***

7: I never married my sweetheart because she wanted to live in the Royal Suite of the New York Waldorf Astoria Hotel and I wanted to live in the Empire State Building!

***

8: I never married my sweetheart because our religions were different!

***

9: I never married my sweetheart because she ate chopped liver in bed and I ate chopped missionary!

***

10: I never married my sweetheart because she hogged the blanket in bed!

***

SUNDAY IN THE PARK WITH *KONG!*

***

Like everyone else in show biz, King Kong has to stay busy with work if he's going to put bread and banana butter on the table! We got to wondering what other films the big ape might make in the future. Here are a few:

KING KONG TAKEOFFS

"KINKY KONG"– Kinky Kong enjoyed being chained up, but escapes from his captors when they refuse to buy him extra-large leather stockings and a beehive wig. He commits a suggestive act with a sky-scraper and finally settles on Fire Island. Rated PG.

***

"KING CON"–Imprisoned for eating a New York City subway train, King Con escapes, kidnaps the warden's daughter, and refuses to give up until officials promise to free "all zoological prisoners" in the dreaded "Big Monkey House." King Con also demands that all inmates are served bananas or coconuts with every meal. Rated X.

***

"KING FU"–King Fu takes on Bruce Lee, the Fighting Dragon Society, an entire karate academy and the Empire State Building in this martial arts-horror flick. The scene in which he smashes the 30th floor of the Empire State Building is superb! Rated R.

***

"SING SONG"–A troupe of unemployed apes during the Depression put together a musical review that pulls a small town out of the doldrums. When the town folk boo the kazoo finale, the apes eat them. Rated PG.

***

"KING KANT"–A philosophical big ape utterly destroys the doctrine of ethical naturalism–along with several skyscrapers and the Holland Tunnel. He also proves that man cannot be happy so long as he still needs dental floss. Rated X.

***

"KING PONG"–In this stunning movie, classic footage of a now classic ground-breaking match between the world's greatest ping-pong champions is interweaved into a new movie of two pong champions — one young, the other old — at the top of their game. When the up-and coming ping pong protégé — a hefty fellow with a lot of hair — loses the critical match, he jumps over the table to congratulate his opponent and accidently crushes him. So it goes. Rated PG.

***

"ESCAPE FROM THE PLANET OF THE PEOPLE'–An ape in search of life in other zip codes crash lands on a planet of hairless beings who try to sell him life insurance and an electric golf cart. He buys the electric golf cart. Rated X.

***

What's big and hairy and climbs up the Empire State Building in a dress?

Queen Kong!

***

LITTLE KNOWN HOLLYWOOD FACT

The whole reason Kong was angry in the "Kong: Skull Island" movie was because no one would call him *King* Kong!

***

KING KONG QUICKIES

Godzilla is the only movie star who blows on the birthday cake to *light* the candles!

***

King Kong uses elephant fertilizer to grow banana trees with *big* trunks!

***

Mothra, flying over King Kong: "Hey. Kong, your hairline has so many peaks and valleys it looks like Skull Island!"

***

I won't say King Kong's Hollywood mansion is cheaply built but when he pulls down the bedroom shade, the mansion comes *down* with it!

***

King Kong oiled all four times on his sports car 'cause they *squeaked* on curves!

***

King Kong's wife is so strong that after she *scrubbed* the floors, Kong came home and fell into the basement!

***

King Kong is so *heavy* that when he rides his horse Kong has to wear roller skates!

***

King Kong doesn't know too much about fine wines — A rich movie producer gave Kong a gift of expensive, fine-aged vintage wine but Kong threw out the bottles because he figured the wine was *stale*!

***

King Kong is a great actor but whoever writes his

movie lines is terrible! I mean, do you remember *anything* Kong said in his movies?

***

King Kong invented *sandpaper suspenders* because he often gets an itchy back!

***

What a New Year's Eve party! At midnight, balloons floated down from the ceiling, the band played Auld Lang Syne, champagne corks popped, the old year passed out, *and so did King Kong!*

***

Have you noticed how *quiet* New Year's Day is? That's because King Kong's wife refuses to speak to Kong!

***

The parking in New York City is so difficult! In fact, it's so difficult that King Kong was overheard telling a cop: "You're giving me a ticket for parking? You should give me a *medal!*"

***

Things sure get confusing. For example, King Kong didn't know what to do when he got back to New York City after spending a few years vacationing on Skull Island. What happened was: Kong finished up a nice dinner with a powerful movie producer at a famous restaurant and when he went to the restroom he saw three doors. The first door had a sign: HIS. The second door had a sign: HERS. And a third door had a sign: *WHATEVER*.

***

King Kong used to work as a bartender in a cheap bar. Every morning, as part of his job, Kong watered the flowers, watered the plants, watered the *liquor!*

***

The bar King Kong used to work in was such a wild place that when a customer came in the door, the bouncer frisked you to check if you had a gun. And if you didn't — the bouncer *gave* you one!

***

King Kong swallowed a weight-loss pill with a sleeping pill so he could take a *light nap!*

***

King Kong has a face only a *Mothra* could love!

***

Mothra kept going to the psychiatrist's office because the *light was on!*

***

King Kong doesn't make British movies because he refuses to carry an *umbrella!*

***

King Kong's agent gets 10% of everything Kong gets except Kong's *ulcer!*

***

Baseball Announcer: "… King Kong just made a great throw—*He threw the second baseman!"*

***

CONTRIBUTORS

Jim Simon is a professional writer. His credits include humor books, adult and YA novels, and pop-culture books. He's still wondering when Kong's agent is going to pay him for this book.

Richard Dominguez is a comic book artist and freelance illustrator/caricaturist. Richard drew the illustrations for this book. He is best known for creating the popular Latino comic book superhero series *El Gato Negro, Nocturnal Warrior.* The series is published through his imprint and art studio, Azteca Productions.

Joe Simon illustrated/painted the book's cover, a parody of promotional art the movie studio used for the 1976 *King Kong* blockbuster. Joe Simon was a legendary comic book artist, writer, inker, editor, and publisher best known for creating *Captain America.*

NOW, IT'S TIME FOR MY
BANANA! 'BYE!!